RULES

of

ENGAGEMENT

Timeless Tips
for
Team Leaders

Joanne L. Smikle

The Practical Press Inc.

Published by The Practical Press Inc.
Simpsonville, MD 21150
www.thepracticalpress.net

Cover and design by SilverBear Graphics
Smikle, Joanne L. *Rules of Engagement: Timeless Tips for Team Leaders*
ISBN 978-0-9709546-5-7

Catalog-in-Publication Data for this book is available from the Library of Congress.
LIBRARY OF CONGRESS CONTROL NUMBER: 2007920747

Dedication

Special thanks to all of the team leaders who continue to enlighten me. I am honored to listen, learn and grow from your examples. Your insightfulness is reflected throughout my work and this book.

Table of Contents

Foreword

Every consultant has a hot topic, a topic that invigorates them. Team building is that topic for me! I love pondering team development. I find it very exciting to examine team dynamics, even team dysfunctions.

Why and how is it that some teams function with the precision of a Swiss watch while others never quite tick? Why are some people more apt to want to serve as team leaders and others want nothing more than to be supportive team members? These are questions I am constantly considering.

I also find the exploration of the skills required for team success fascinating. There are specific competencies that guarantee success in a collaborative environment. Since we all know that there is a definite skill set, why don't we develop it? That's another interesting question.

This book reflects my never-ending quest for answers to these and other questions about smart collaboration. It is one of many contributions that I intend to make to the body of usable knowledge about teams, team leadership and related areas. I hope you enjoy reading it as much as I enjoyed writing it.

Introduction

Whether you are a team member who wants to move into the team leader role or are already managing a team or workgroup, this book contains useful tips that you can implement to be more successful. This is the third in a series of three books on collaboration. The first, *Calamity-Free Collaboration: Making Teamwork WORK!*, provides practical tools for building a team oriented workplace. It is a useful guide for any organization that wants to create a collaborative culture. This first book presents action planning tools, assessments and real world case studies. The second, *Rules of Engagement: Timeless Tips for Teams*, addresses people, processes and products. It provides everything that you need to deal with the human element, the processes that people use and how to get people to consistently deliver the highest quality outputs.

This third book is designed to give you real tools that you can use to maximize your effectiveness in the leadership role. It is divided into three sections: *Individual*, *Interpersonal* and *Organizational*. The first section, *Individual*, highlights specific competencies that you need to demonstrate. This section will help you harness your unique abilities and channel them in the direction that best benefits a collaborative workplace. The second section, *Interpersonal*, covers the activities required to get the best from your team members. This section helps you examine your human relations abilities. It also enables you to connect your personal approach to creating high functioning interpersonal dynamics on the team. The final section, *Organizational*, helps you manage the team's work in the larger organization. It addresses organizational dynamics and organizational development.

Use this book as a reference for your own professional development. Each of the rules presented can be used as a developmental objective. You can identify a set objective to tackle each month. The three sections are followed by developmental worksheets designed to help you begin using the rules immediately.

Section One

INDIVIDUAL

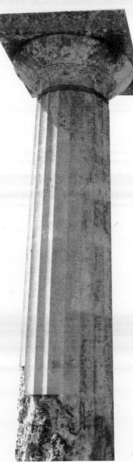

Individual
Rules of Engagement

Rule #1:   Give feedback

Rule #2:   Reward

Rule #3:   Be a catalyst for change

Rule #4:   Start out like you want to
             hold out

Rule #5:   Have a strategic focus

Rule #6:   Develop mastery

Rule #7:   Stand for something

Rule #8:   Tend to your own
             professional development

Rule #9:   Protect

Rule #10:   Reflect

Rule #11:   Recognize constraints

Rule #12:   Identify impediments
             to collaboration

Rule #13:   Check your ego at the door

Rule #14:   Respond

Rule #1: Give feedback

Team members need to hear how well they are performing. They also need to get straight information on areas where they need to grow. Giving feedback can make you uncomfortable if you are typically conflict avoidant. You may feel that feedback is fertile ground for strife, conflict and even confusion. Those feelings are a sure sign that you need to rethink how you handle this developmental conversation.

There are many models for giving people feedback. Begin with the positive. It is best delivered in the most timely manner possible. In other words, catch people doing things right and tell them about it on the spot. When team members produce great work, tell them. When they go the extra mile, thank them. Praise can be public or private. Know your team members well enough to learn whether they prefer private praise or public.

When giving correctional feedback, begin the process by adjusting your mindset. Consider it an opportunity to promote personal and professional development—theirs and yours. Consider this prime time for building stronger communication bridges with individuals on the team. Begin the process before the actual interaction. Here's a formula that works well:

- Figure out your reservations…what are you dreading?

- What are the primary objectives of the conversation?

- What are the outcomes you seek?

- How can you deliver the message in a manner that will make the team member receptive?

- What is the best time and place to have this conversation?

- How will you engage the team member in the conversation?

- When you seek their input, how will you validate it or incorporate it into solution generation?

- How will you monitor the outcomes?

- How will you test for the team member's understanding?

- How will you follow-up?

Feedback is most likely to be well-received when it is specific, reflects an observed behavior or pattern of behaviors and is as objective as possible. Use "I" messages. For example, "Mary, I have noticed that you have been late turning in the last three reports. Help me understand what's going on." This approach cites an unambiguous example of pattern behavior. It is not attacking and it offers the team member an opportunity to share their perspective. The same approach can be used when providing praise. For example, "Juan I am so pleased with how detailed your analyses are. They really help us make well-informed decisions. Thanks for the great work!" In either case be precise and sincere.

The other critical piece of providing feedback is listening to the team member's response. It will give you insight into their perspectives, problems and ideas. Listening is another strong bridge-building tool. Hearing other perspectives helps you better understand how team members are experiencing their work, the team and the larger organization.

Rule #2: Reward

Catching people doing things right and providing feedback are the basics. The next step is providing rewards. Rewards can include anything from a sincere thank you note, time off, money or gift certificates. Check-in with team members to find out what types of rewards hold the most meaning for them. Rewards, like feedback, need to be delivered in a timely manner and have significance to the receiver. They must also be given based on merit, not just warm, fuzzy feelings. Behavior that gets rewarded gets repeated. Be very careful that you are rewarding the right behavior.

Rule #3: Be a catalyst for change

Team members are looking to your for guidance and direction. This includes guidance not only on the projects, but also on attitude. Understand the vital role that you play in creating change. If innovation becomes a norm for you, it will become a norm for your team members. Being a catalyst for change requires you to not only talk about flexibility, but to actually model a willingness to adapt. Serving as a change agent means that you have to be open to different ideas and approaches, whether they fit with your traditional thoughts or not. We all have mental preconceptions that we apply without really considering alternative approaches. As a catalyst for change you will move from autopilot to more thoughtful methods.

Rule #4: Start out like you want to hold out

Behave in a consistent manner. Begin with integrity, innovation and commitment. Keep those behaviors alive in every interaction. This enables you to establish a reputation for excellence. It also supports and sustains your role as a catalyst for change. You are already viewed in a positive light because you began by putting your very best forward. Consistently admirable behavior is bound to produce consistently admirable results.

Rule #5: Have a strategic focus

The organization's strategy is the essential guide for any and every meaningful activity. In order for you to support your organization's strategy, you must first understand it. Once you understand that strategy, you are then able to explain it to your team. Strategy is then connected to every activity you lead. Many team leaders make the mistake of getting wrapped up in the projects and the processes without understanding how they are connected to the larger organization's strategy.

Having a strategic focus also means that you will adhere to deadlines. When you understand strategy, you understand why it is important to do things well and to do them in a timely manner. Comprehending strategy helps you comprehend the fact that your work does not happen in a vacuum.

You understand that not only is your work important, but it also impacts other areas of the organization.

Rule #6: Develop mastery

Mastery, the ability to move beyond mediocrity to substantive knowledge, is one of the make or break abilities for any leader. Your team is looking to you for your expertise. They are looking to you for guidance as they develop a greater breadth and depth of knowledge. Building mastery means that you are committed to learning. You are responsible for learning about the work of the larger organization, the work of the business units that your team's products impact, and the projects of each team member.

Mastery is a journey. It is a never ending path paved by intellectual curiosity. Levels of mastery evolve as we learn new information, gain insights from others and integrate our knowledge into the work of the team and the larger organization. Mastery is not just about learning. It is about testing, implementation and evaluation. Once you have developed substantial knowledge in one area, your mastery is tested by where and how you can apply that knowledge. Knowledge without integration is not true mastery, it is simply learning.

Rule #7: Stand for something

The courage of your convictions will distinguish you (and your team) in your company and even in your industry. Having the guts to stand up and be counted may be tough at first, but that courage will help you garner resources for your team. It is that same courage that will enable you to deliver the feedback mentioned in Rule #1.

A word of caution: select your battles carefully. A courageous fool is of little value to themselves or the company. Think seriously about the stand that you want to take, whether it is consistent with your core values and the results you anticipate. This thoughtful consideration will help you carefully analyze whether the view is worth the climb.

Rule #8: Tend to your own professional development

Growing is essential! Make time for learning, exploring and other forms of intellectual curiosity. The more that you as the leader know, the more able you will be to inspire the on-going development of your team members.

Consider using any number of resources for your growth. You may decide to subscribe to Harvard Business Review. This publication covers contemporary business topics with depth and insight. You may decide to avail yourself to the resources offered by your trade or professional association. These organizations offer the most recent information about trends specific to your marketplace. Another by-product of association activities is that you build a network of like-minded colleagues interested in learning, growth and professional development. Of course you can also attend training and education offered within your company. These activities will help you build a strong internal network.

Rule #9: Protect

Every business, whether in the public or private sector, whether for profit or nonprofit, has organizational politics. They are inevitable. As a leader you are responsible for not allowing every issue to impact your team. Vent with your peers, not with your team members. Don't use your team members as your therapists or confessors. Get those needs met in other places. While your team members will certainly be aware of what is going on in the company, they need not be bothered with each and every pressure that you face.

Rule #10: Reflect

An action orientation is essential; however, that action needs to be planned and purposeful. Ensure that your plan and purpose are clearly reflected in your actions by taking the time to reflect before engaging. In addition to reflecting prior to action, make the time to reflect as you are learning. Tending to your professional development will give you abundant new, useful information to reflect on and then integrate.

You must also encourage that same level of introspection from team members. Instead of always pushing for immediate or rushed decisions, give people time to process ideas and then synthesize them with what they already know. As you and team members are reflecting, be sure to have discussions.

Reflection with discussion allows everyone to expand their knowledge base and broaden their perspectives.

Rule #11: Recognize constraints

Life has limitations. The work world has limitations. As individuals we have personal limitations; it is a fact of life. Be clear with yourself about your organizational constraints. While you may want to build the Taj Mahal, you may not be able to do it on the city block allocated to you. Constraints also include resources. While your team may need a seven figure budget, you may be allocated less. Be realistic. Make the best of your resources.

In addition to financial constraints, there are always human constraints. If you need specialized resources and don't have them on your team, be creative. Hire interns. Borrow staff from other departments. Recognize the constraints and then work your way around them.

Rule #12: Identify impediments to collaboration

There is always something or someone that gets in the way of teamwork. Some of the obstacles center around distance. It is hard to work as a team when everyone telecommutes. It can be tough when the team is spread in various locations across the nation. Some obstacles revolve around people and personality. There are always a few cantankerous critters in every workplace. Some raise the level of

IDENTIFYING IMPEDIMENTS TO COLLABORATION

Impediment	Nature of Impediment	Potential Strategies for Overcoming Impediment

conflict, others impede progress on projects. Yet other impediments involve processes. This happens when team processes are unclear, overly complex or simply inadequate. Whatever your unique impediment, be careful to make the time to identify it so that you can then attack the problem.

There are other obstacles outside of the team. They may include organizational politics. Reality shows us that politics abound in any and every organization. The can be minor impediments or they can be quite major. Scarce resources are another possible impediment. It is difficult to get anything accomplished when you don't have the talent, technology or time. This is another reality of life that you will need to find ways to overcome.

You must first identify impediments before you can move beyond them. Once you have identified these potential stumbling blocks, determine their nature. Do they revolve around people, policies, practices or procedures? This will help you plot a course for going over, around or through the obstacle. It is also quite useful to tentatively identify ways to get past the impediment. The chart that follows gives you a framework for tackling your impediments.

Rule #13: Check your ego at the door

The team project is the most important endeavor. While you may be absolutely brilliant, your brilliance is not nearly as important as the work of the team. When your ego rears its ugly head, remember that you are not the source of all knowledge. Each team member brings something important to the table. Draw on their intelligence and experience.

Rule #14: Respond

Effective team leaders should be responsive even when responses require research and a tight timeline. Be willing to admit when you don't have an answer, and then get the information as quickly as possible. Follow-up while you are getting information so that the other person knows you have not forgotten. This applies to your interactions with colleagues at all levels.

Responsiveness also applies to work with your team members. Be open to their questions. Make every effort to answer and provide the additional resources required. Respond to all inquiries, even those that make you uncomfortable. We often shy away from what we perceive as confrontational. Those are just the inquiries that you must acknowledge and address. Failing to do this will undermine your credibility and raise suspicions about your competence.

Section One
Practical Applications

My developmental objective for implementing the Rules of Engagement listed in the first section:

This objective is linked to which Rule(s)?

I selected this objective because…

Potential action steps for making my objective reality…

Results of implementation of each action steps…

Key learnings…

Section Two
INTERPERSONAL

Interpersonal
Rules of Engagement

Rule #15:   Garner commitment, not mere compliance

Rule #16:   Create inclusion

Rule #17:   Set the stage for success

Rule #18:   Be willing to concede your role

Rule #19:   Commit to regular reality checks

Rule #20:   Align behaviors with core values

Rule #21:   Build the capacity for change

Rule #22:   Demonstrate commitment

Rule #23:   Publicize successes

Rule #24:   Help create constructive core values

Rule #25:   Link core values to team values

Rule #26:   Create continuity

Rule #27:   Lead the team in education and training

Rule #28:   Promote healthy interdependence

Rule #29:   Promote accountability

Rule #30:   Balance task and relational elements

Rule #31:   Create a sense of belonging for all members

Rule #32:   Coach for peak performance

Rule #15: Garner commitment, not mere compliance

Compliance is simply doing the job because you must. There is little enthusiasm or investment beyond what is minimally required. Commitment implies a sincere desire to do the work and do it well. Commitment is inspired by any number of factors. It can be inspired by a compelling corporate mission. Noble work regulated by high standards creates an environment where commitment is compelling. Commitment can also be inspired by a charismatic leader. Leaders who have magnetic, charming personalities can inspire commitment by virtue of their interpersonal competence. Commitment is inspired by healthy work environments where free communication is the norm. When people feel free to express themselves they are more apt to invest in the workplace because they know that not only are they heard, but their opinions are sought and valued.

Rule #16: Create inclusion

Build a team with diverse members representing the different operational units in the organization. Draw out different ideas and opinions, whether they are consistent with yours or not. Incorporate that diversity in your processes and products.

Creating inclusion goes beyond having representation from different functional units, it includes creating an environment where human diversity is the norm. This means that your team will reflect the variety of people in the larger organization. This means that you will be inclusive of different races, genders (there are only two, so that will not be hard), educational levels, sexual orientations and so on. The workplace is comprised of so many different people, your team should be a positive reflection of that rich mixture.

Rule #17: Set the stage for success

Seek supporters in the organization. Gather the resources that are required. Begin by collaboratively creating a process that will work for your team. This includes tentative plans for how you will make decisions, address conflicts and hold each other accountable. Setting the stage also includes defining roles and responsibilities. You, as well as every other team member, need clarity on what you are supposed to do, why and how. Establishing this type of clarity in the beginning saves time, energy and frustration. It is the front end work that enables enduring team success!

Rule #18: Be willing to concede your role

My grandmother used to say that a good run beats a bad stand. If you find that you are in over your head, don't be afraid to walk away and make room for another leader. Everyone is not good at everything, so be clear about whether you are ready and able to lead.

Beginning with readiness, people are often promoted simply because they have done a job well for many years. Technical proficiency does not make a leader. If you question your own leadership skills consider taking small bites. Perhaps you can lead an element of a project instead of the entire project. This will give you the opportunity to build both your abilities and your confidence. Moving to abilities, if you know that your leadership skills are lackluster, let someone else have the job. I have a very honest colleague who readily admits that she doesn't grasp strategic issues. This makes her a poor choice for team leader on projects that require a strategic focus. Knowing your strengths and weaknesses gives you factual information for deciding whether or not a leadership role is right for you.

Rule #19: Commit to regular reality checks

Fantasies are fun! Fiction is a wonderful escape! Neither will help you or your team move to maximum performance. Not only do you have a responsibility to perform reality checks on your own abilities, but you also have to guide the team in conducting their own. A sample team leader assessment instrument follows. Use it to conduct reality checks on your performance.

Rule #20: Align behaviors with core values

What do you believe in? What do you, at the core of your being, believe to be a truth? What are the essential components of your character? Take the time to answer these questions. They reveal your core values. When you answer them you may come up with things like honesty and integrity as core values. You may come up with hard work, sacrifice and humility. A focus on family, maintaining

REALITY CHECK FOR TEAM LEADERS

Use this tool to measure your effectiveness as a team leader. Answer candidly with complete honesty. Use the *Current* column to indicate your current proficiency. Use the *Desired* column to indicate your desired proficiency. The rating scale follows:

1	2	3	4
Never	*Infrequently*	*Regularly*	*Always*

People	Current	Desired
Team members speak with me candidly about their opinions, even when those opinions are different from mine		
I consistently work to build networks throughout the company and throughout the industry		
I am comfortable with conflict and use appropriate approaches to reach satisfactory resolution		
I make it a point to coach my team on the positive and negative to ensure consistent performance		

Process	Current	Desired
I make sure that we audit our processes so that they are effective and efficient		
I promote inclusion in ways that make our processes cooperative and collaborative		
Our processes are refined enough to adequately tackle our tasks but no so complex as to be a burden		
While we take the time to be thorough, I do not allow the team to get bogged down in analysis, unproductive discussions or indecision		

Product	Current	Desired
I make sure that our products (or outputs) go through rigorous quality control checks so that they meet customer expectations		
We are flexible enough to quickly modify products (or outputs) when our customers ask us to		
I make sure that the team understands where our outputs fit in with, support or supplement work in other parts of the organization		
Before we develop a product or deliver an output we make sure that it reflects the competitive intelligence gathered from competitors, customers and other stakeholders		

meaningful relationships and connectedness may surface as your critical values.

Whatever your values, your behavior should be congruent. Your decisions should reflect the beliefs that you hold true. Your relationships will colleagues must also reflect these principles. This alignment benefits you, your team and everyone else that you encounter. People know what to expect from you. They know that you will be consistent. More important, you will not experience a feeling of hypocrisy or deceit. You will know that everything you do is clearly aligned with who are at your core.

This type of principle-based alignment occurs when our values are consistent with the organization's values. When we believe in the mission, values and strategic intent of the enterprise, we are more likely to experience a connectedness and congruence. Alignment between your values and your actions is the first step. The next step is being certain that you are working in an organization where your beliefs are consistent with those of the organization. Absent congruence, you will be working at cross-purposes internally and within the larger context of your organization.

Rule #21: Build the capacity for change

Building your own capacity for change occurs when you understand that change is a process, not an event. It happens when you understand your reactions to change and can channel those reactions into positive action. The next step is to help team members understand the dynamics of change, how change impacts them and how to channel their energy. Team members look to you for guidance in tumultuous times. They look to you for direction. Be sure to introduce change in small, manageable chunks. Overwhelming people with everything at once will only frustrate them. Using small increments allows team members to build a record of success with innovation. These successes help them develop mastery on which to continue building.

Building the capacity for change also necessitates an understanding of how human beings adapt. There will be team members who are eager to jump on board. They view change as a positive opportunity. There will be others who have healthy skepticism. They will consider the change, weigh the pros and cons, and then decide to give it a try. There are still others who will present cynicism. These are the people who are fearful of change, reluctant to try new approaches and stuck in a mode that may not be beneficial to the team.

Of course no person falls exclusively into one category all of the time. Most of us respond depending on the change, what it will mean to us and our work and the results we anticipate. Your job is to understand their fears and communicate with them to clarify the change. You are also responsible for maintaining open lines of communication so that team members feel comfortable discussing alternatives, methods of implementation and whatever other issues they are experiencing.

CHANGE...

- Isn't always welcomed
- Impacts people before systems, services, products and processes
- Requires developmental growth because each step is harder than the step before
- Seldom happens without periods of reversion and resistance
- Requires consistent commitment accompanied by clear communication

---

Rule #22: Demonstrate commitment

Commitment is your pledge to lead the team in the direction that supports the organization in the pursuit of its unique purpose. It can be demonstrated in any number of ways. You can show your commitment by building bridges with stakeholders, by carrying your share of the load and by coaching team members.

Commitment is shown through the language and imagery that you use to describe the work and the workplace. Do you use positive language? Do you question in search of solutions? Do you affirm the worth of your work and your company? If your language is positive and your behavior is aligned with it, your commitment will be evident. This is not to say that you will never complain or be discouraged, rather that you will channel those emotions into a positive direction.

Rule #23: Publicize successes

Let's face facts, humility can be overrated. Decision makers need to know when your team hits a homerun. They will certainly know when you strike out. It is your job, and that of every team member, to let stakeholders know when you have succeeded, how that success was created and how it benefits the larger organization.

You can publicize successes in any number of ways. Use your company's intranet to share best practices. Consider discussing your successes at department meetings. If there are internal newsletters, use them to document milestones and accomplishments. One other way to get your successes noticed is to write articles on your unique approaches, how they have benefited the company and applications in the industry. Editors of your professional association's journals will love you forever. They are always looking for relevant content. This boosts the reputation of your company and your team. It also adds to the body of usable knowledge in your industry.

Rule #24: Help create constructive core values

Just as your core values need to clarified, so to do those of your team members. Many people have never considered why they act the way they act, and as a result they operate in a state of unconscious incompetence. This is when people don't know *that* they don't know and they don't know *what* they don't know. Clarifying values is the first step on the knowledge journey. As team leader it is your job to create a constructive environment for personal growth. Begin with your own clarification and then move to the level of helping others develop the same clarity.

Rule #25: Link core values to team values

Once your core values and those of the team have been clarified, you will then be able to align the work. Linkages between core values and team values must be clear. If one of the values that your team accepts is a commitment to quality, everyone must be held to the highest standards. Not only will they be held to those standards by each other, they will also be guided by an internal commitment. If one of the values is a commitment to innovation, then every team member will be encouraged to suggest, test and try new ideas.

By the same token, when core values are not linked to team values, a helter-skelter culture erupts. Team members are acting in ways that resonate with them as individuals but not necessarily with the team. Customers don't have any idea of what to expect from the team because the sense of identity, interdependence and purpose is not clearly defined.

Rule #26: Create continuity

Team members may come and go depending on retention, career rotations and other factors. As they shift in and out, new members need to be oriented about the team's work, processes and values. They also need to know their role, the role of others and how their responsibilities are interconnected. Members also need to know the key stakeholders and the expectations of the team. All of this information builds both clarity and continuity.

Rule #27: Lead the team in education and training

All education need not be external. As team leader you can keep the learning cycle going. Training does not have to be long or arduous. Use short modules to target specific developmental areas. Topics can include problem solving, meeting management, conflict management, communication skills, team development, process management, project management, team evaluation, work flow and process analysis, presentation skills, budgeting, financial management, influencing others, etc. Just as you can lead the learning, so can team members. Encourage them to share their special knowledge, to build new knowledge and, most of all, to share the learning.

Other useful forms of learning include video-based training, case studies and assessments. Each of these tools must be customized to meet the developmental needs of the team. They must address relevant developmental objectives.

Rule #28: Promote healthy interdependence

Since we know that no one of us is as smart as all of us, it is up to you to connect team members and their work. Help every member understand how their work connects with the work of others. Encourage them to rely not just on themselves, not just on you, but on each other. Whenever possible, pair up team members to tackle projects. This will help them develop an appreciation of each other's expertise.

Rule #29: Promote accountability

Behavior that gets rewarded gets repeated. We only measure that which matters. Both of these phrases allude to the necessity of accountability. As a leader holding people accountable is one of your primary responsibilities. This means tracking deadlines, quality and customer satisfaction. It also means that you will coach team members when they are having trouble measuring up. You are also responsible for coaching them when things are going well. This recognition keeps team members encouraged. Accountability applies to you as well. Be certain that you are holding yourself to the same high standards.

As standards change, you are responsible for communicating that information to team members and stakeholders. It is difficult to hold people to standards that are constantly changing. It is even more difficult when the standards are vague, unclear or ambiguous. Be sure that you are talking about your expectations, customer requirements and the like. Allow the conversation to flow with team members asking you questions and sharing their perceptions.

Rule #30: Balance task and relational elements

The work is important, and so is the fun. Put sufficient time into fostering strong relationships with your team members, customers and other stakeholders. These informal relationships are how your support systems will not only develop, but flourish.

Rule #31: Create a sense of belonging for all members

Because of the diversity of team members, customers and the entire organization, it is imperative that leaders make everyone feel like a valued member of the group. This means fostering open communication, allowing conflict and ensuring that every voice is heard. Creating a sense of belonging means that you pay attention to all elements of team interactions, from communication to process to conflict resolution. How the team handles each of these activities will determine whether members feel that they are respected as part of the whole or whether they feel marginalized and ostracized.

A sense of belonging also generates a higher level of commitment to the team and the company. When people feel that they matter in and to the group, they are willing to invest. They will also be more willing to demonstrate their commitment with hard work and dedication. Team members will do more when they are assured that they are valued members of a high performing workgroup.

Rule #32: Coach for peak performance

Excellent performance does not happen by accident. It is the result of commitment in word and deed. This means not only individual commitment, but commitment from a coach. As the team leader you are that coach. Coaching is the developmental relationship characterized by reflection, behavioral observations, candid feedback and supportive guidance towards higher levels of performance. Coaching is a developmental process, not an evaluative one. It is the component of the performance management process that builds constant dialogue aimed at delivering the best results.

COACHING IS...

The developmental process used to reinforce excellent performance and correct negative. Successful coaches ably coach individuals and teams. They use candid, caring communication to provide feedback. Coaching is an integral component of the performance management process though it not used for evaluation.

Being a skillful coach requires practice. You must practice good listening skills. Your relationships will be strengthened by the ability to hear and understand diverse perspectives. This will also garner the respect of whomever you coach. They will know, from your listening, that you are interested in their growth. You must also practice providing constructive feedback. This means providing feedback about a person's strengths and weaknesses. All too often managers use coaching as a tool only for addressing deficient behaviors. In fact, it is an excellent way to reinforce the positive. You will also have to practice providing gentle guidance without going overboard and micromanaging. Guidance entails leading by example and making suggestions. It also entails collaboration in establishing goals and objectives. As the coaching team leader you are also responsible for setting parameters and standards. You will have to be clear about the parameters while allowing people to exercise their unique creativity within those guidelines. It is in that exercise of creativity that people realize their full potential. As coach you are in a prime position to lead people on the process to self-discovery.

Section Two
Practical Applications

My developmental objective for implementing the Rules of Engagement listed in the second section:

This objective is linked to which Rule(s)?

I selected this objective because...

Potential action steps for making my objective reality...

Results of implementation of each action steps...

Key learnings...

Section Three
ORGANIZATIONAL

Organizational
Rules of Engagement

Rule #33:   Disturb the status quo

Rule #34:   Provide an organizational context for the team's work

Rule #35:   Align the team's work with core business objectives

Rule #36:   Challenge unproductive norms, values and behaviors

Rule #37:   Engage throughout the organization

Rule #38:   Implement innovative strategies

Rule #39:   Get external expertise

Rule #40:   Build influence

Rule #41:   Use problem-solving skills

Rule #42:   Encourage organizational development

Rule #43:   Create external linkages

Rule #44:   Identify and secure critical resources

Rule #45:   Ensure that strategies and processes support equity

Rule #46:   Scan the environment to identify opportunities

Rule #33: Disturb the status quo

Shake it up! Mix it up! Move it around! Team leadership, and leadership in general, require you to launch innovative, interesting initiatives that move the organization closer to its goals. Getting there (wherever 'there' is for your company) calls for action, movement and occasional disruptions. Progress cannot happen without disturbances.

As a leader you are responsible for the disturbances and disruptions. They need to be purposeful, calculated and targeted. The disturbances also need to be synchronized with the organization's strategic intent. This synchronization ensures alignment. Remember, be conscious of the human responses to change. Everyone will not be thrilled with what they perceive as interruptions to their work.

Rule #34: Provide an organizational context for the team's work

Your work does not happen in a vacuum. It happens in the context of a larger organization that may have what appear to be competing or conflicting goals. Take the time to connect the dots for team members. Help them understand how each project and each individual contribution supports the larger organization. This instills people with a sense of purpose. It also provides answers to many of the questions, spoken and unspoken, about the rationale for decisions.

Once team members understand how their efforts connect to other areas of the organization, they will be more able to build rapport with stakeholders. Team members will have the knowledge to communicate with colleagues throughout the company about substantive business issues. Their products will also evolve because of their understanding of how much the work matters.

Rule #35: Align the team's work with core business objectives

Just as the team needs to understand their labor in the larger organizational context, they need to be clear about the business objectives that guide their work. Business objectives will vary depending on the needs of stakeholders. Your customers may be driven by industry changes, resource constraints or new developments in research. Whatever the drivers, they translate into specific business objectives. Help team members understand those objectives. Build your own understanding by having frequent contact with stakeholders so that you have in-depth comprehension of their objectives. Be flexible. Understand that their objectives cannot remain constant; they will change and evolve based on many different variables.

Rule #36: Challenge unproductive norms, values and behaviors

How team members act and interact is both a reflection of them and you. Their behavior reflects what they have learned, practiced and refined. If they are collaborative, supportive and communicative, it is because those behaviors have been ingrained. The reverse is also true. If members are overly competitive, malcontent and deceptive, it is because those behaviors have been perfected through practice.

So, how does their behavior become a reflection of you, the leader? When you allow the negative behavior to go unchecked, it becomes both pervasive and contagious. That happens because you let it happen by failing to hold people accountable. By the same token, if you reward and recognize positive behavior, that behavior will become normative for the team.

The role that values and norms play in collaborative interactions is critical. Values are the accepted set of beliefs of the team, its work, its customers and the larger organization. While every member may not be in total agreement, you must all share the majority of your core beliefs. If these beliefs are not shared, you wind up creating a level of dissonance that will eventually surface in unproductive ways. Your values directly impact the norms. Norms are simply how you agree to work together. Productive norms include an agreement to build consensus when making decisions, adhering

INNOVATION IS...

♦ The deliberate search for unusual solutions

♦ Reliant on ingenuity, creativity and a little imagination

♦ Easier said than done

♦ Contingent upon the willingness to share, test and tinker with ideas

♦ Most successful when focused on one specific target rather than many different areas

to schedules, communicating through conflict and respect for the customer. It is up to you to foster meaningful, substantive norms. Both you and your team members are responsible for monitoring adherence.

Rule #37: Engage throughout the organization

Engaging necessitates more than skillful politicking. It is more than politely accommodating the needs of colleagues. Engaging entails showing genuine interest in your colleague's work. It also means providing resources and support for their struggles. Lend an ear. Equally as important, lend a hand. These are signs of significant engagement.

Engagement is also shown when you don't sabotage, whether consciously or unconsciously, the work of other teams. Make sure that your work coordinates and compliments other efforts in the company. This will require you to have discussions with other leaders about what they are working on. When you have conflicting or competing agendas put the issues on the table. Find ways to work together wherever possible.

Rule #38: Implement innovative strategies

Take it upon yourself to stay abreast of new approaches to your work. It is also wise to stay current on cutting edge approaches in your industry. If you are keenly aware of relevant trends, you can then share that knowledge with your team members. Once new ideas are on the table they can be put to the test.

Turn your innovative approaches into best practices by monitoring implementation. Keep track of exactly how your team was able to apply specific principles of the new approach, what other areas of the business were impacted by the innovation and the results at each stage of the process. Additionally, it is helpful to track costs, resources allocated and resources required.

Rule #39: Get external expertise

You cannot do everything yourself, nor can you know everything. Reach out and draw on the experience of others. Do not be embarrassed by what you don't know. Be humble enough to recognize your knowledge gaps and enlist the assistance of other bright people to fill those gaps. This does not only mean the expertise of external consultants. It also means soliciting internal expertise. Your company has a knowledge bank of which you (and every other leader) should avail yourselves.

When seeking external expertise, be clear about what you need, how and when you need it. Provide a context for the work or knowledge you are seeking. This context includes how the information fits into the work of the team, other related data that you already have, how all of the information will be used and other salient information.

Rule #40: Build influence

Leadership, by definition, is one's ability to influence. That influence is exercised both vertically and horizontally. In other words, as a leader you are

OASIS©
Problem Solving Model

Origin

Acknowledge & Analyze

Search for Solutions

Input on Implementation

Satisfaction with Solutions

able to influence everyone from your peer group, bosses, and staff. Building influence begins with the clarity previously mentioned. Once you are clear about your core values and the principles that guide your behavior, you can behave congruently. That consistent behavior builds a positive reputation. Developing the ability to listen, reflect and offer suggestions when asked are other key components of influence. Rather than prattling on and on about your thoughts and ideas, use your time to digest information provided by others.

Another way to build influence is to contribute to your profession. These contributions can take on many different forms. You can write for your industry publications. You can volunteer to serve on industry councils and task forces. Consider becoming active in your professional association. Consider using your expertise to develop interesting presentations for industry conferences. There are any number of ways that you can build both influence and credibility.

Rule #41: Use problem-solving skills

The ability to dismantle, untangle, dissect and otherwise analyze is what problem-solving is all about. Getting to workable solutions is what most of us focus on; however, the process by which those solutions are born is worthy of exploration. While there are many different problem solving models, try the OASIS© model. It is a simple model that you can apply to a myriad of situations on your team and within the larger organization.

Each stage of this model allows active participation by everyone involved in the problem. Because the model works equally well as an approach to problem solving and conflict resolution, the terms may be used interchangeably in this section. It is collaborative in nature, thereby allowing each person to have ownership in solutions and resolution. The first stage, *Origin*, begins the search for the root of the problem. In this stage there is an active search, brainstorming works well, for the origin. This search will yield information on whether the conflict is rooted in values, beliefs, power, control, position or some other factor. The *Origin* stage is where everyone involved gets clear on exactly what they are facing. This eliminates the tendency to jump in and search for solutions to symptoms and not to the actual problem.

Moving on to *Acknowledge & Analyze*... At this stage all parties acknowledge the existence and impact of the problem, as well as the agreed upon origins. This is when you discuss the impact the conflict has on individuals, the team and the larger organization. Make a clear connection between acceptable standards, mission, values and other guiding principles that govern your organization.

Allow everyone to share their interpretations of the problem, then you can begin collaborating on thorough analysis. The analysis should include the impact that the conflict has on all stakeholders.

You have laid the foundation. It is time to start the *Search for Solutions*. Set boundaries, identify limits and parameters. This is important because some solutions will not be feasible. Rather than allowing people to travel down an inappropriate road, give them the framework for generating solutions.

Use this search as an opportunity to exchange ideas about what may solve the problem. Solutions may be very simple or quite complex. Either way, generate as many possible solutions as possible. Make sure that everyone has an understanding of the solutions being considered. This will make it easier for people to make well-informed decisions when it is time to select a course of action.

It is now time to get *Input on Implementation*. Boundaries need to be restated. Develop a clear draft of an implementation plan. The plan must address the root of the conflict. Identify all of the key players, especially customers. Make sure that there is a clear connection between the solutions goals and objectives that define strategy and operations in the company.

Now that you have defined or at least drafted an implementation plan, it is important to identify monitoring techniques. How will you and everyone else stay on track? Think of ways to track performance, productivity, systems and services related to your solution. It is vital that you track every aspect of the solution so that you know whether it is sufficient.

The last stage of the process is *Satisfaction with Solutions*. It can only happen after you have been using the implementation plan. This phase of the model allows you to use the tracking techniques designed earlier. By using them you will have no problem discussing progress in an honest, constructive format. Use this as the opportunity to modify solutions so they more adequately address the problem.

Rule #42: Encourage organizational development

Organizational development is the process used to strengthen the talent-base, the systems related to people and the overall performance of people throughout the enterprise. It encompasses everything from education, training, succession planning, recruitment and retention to career pathing. As team leader you have an inherent responsibility to work towards the organization's long-term growth. This involves working to ensure the professional development of each team member. Their growth ensures organizational growth.

Rule #43: Create external linkages

Of course you will be forming partnerships and networks with people outside of the team. They may turn into great sources of resources, talent, ideas and feedback. But, these linkages go farther than that. Build a network with colleagues in other organizations. They may have best practices that can inform your team's work. Form linkages with leaders in professional associations. They will have the latest facts on trends in your industry. They will also offer educational opportunities for you and your team members.

Rule #44: Identify and secure critical resources

Would you drive your car if you knew it was out of gas? Would you try to bake a cake if you knew you were out of flour? Would you travel abroad without a passport? Of course not! These preposterous examples illustrate just how silly it is to have your team working without the resources necessary for them to accomplish tasks and deliver high quality outcomes. As team leader it is up to you work hard to be sure that resources are at the team's disposal. These resources can include anything from administrative support to technology to training to access to senior executives. Whatever resources are required, be sure that your team has enough of them.

Rule #45: Ensure that strategies and processes support equity

We don't intend to create inequalities on our teams. But, our subconscious mind leads us to be more lenient to the people we like. When we feel a kindred spirit we are more likely to subtly give preferential treatment. It is not our intent to establish double standards, but that is often the result.

These same unconscious preferences can impact the strategies and processes we support. We may endorse more sound approaches that benefit favored customers or stakeholders. We may bend or break rules when they seem to encumber those same folks. And the reverse may also be true. We may be subconsciously inclined to do less for problem stakeholders. Ensure equity by paying close attention to your approach, both strategic and operational, with all team members and stakeholders.

Rule #46: Scan the environment to identify opportunities

Once your team has established a solid track record, search for new opportunities that call for more skill. Get in the habit of volunteering for additional assignments. Encourage team members to be on the search for opportunities too. When scanning the environment you will continue to have in-depth conversations with people in your network. They will know about activities on the horizon. They may also be able to steer your team in new and challenging directions.

Section Three
Practical Applications

My developmental objective for implementing the Rules of Engagement listed in the third section:

This objective is linked to which Rule(s)?

I selected this objective because…

Potential action steps for making my objective reality…

Results of implementation of each action steps…

Key learnings…

Summary

You now have forty-six more tools to maximize your leadership effectiveness. The individual competencies, consistently applied, will help you tap your unique abilities. You can then use your strengths to build a collaborative workplace. The interpersonal competencies give you what you need to get team members to maximize their input. Employ the tips in this second section to hone your human relations skills. These tips enable you to use your individual style to dramatically improve interpersonal dynamics on the team. The organizational competencies provide you with practical approaches to connecting the team's work to the larger organization. Building your expertise in this area will help you understand organizational dynamics and organizational development.

This book is a tool for on-going professional development. Use the Practical Applications after each section to stay focused on skill-building. Not only will you be able to use the tips, you will develop your own insights. The combination of the tips and your unique approaches will make you a most engaging team leader.

About the Author

Joanne L. Smikle is a respected consultant, author and speaker. She devises practical strategies that promote sustained change in corporate culture while enhancing performance and productivity. Joanne's systematic approaches effectively address long-term developmental needs. She helps her clients build the competencies required to meet and exceed business demands.

Joanne uses the market intelligence gained through research-based consulting to create captivating keynotes for corporations and associations. She facilitates retreats, workshops and educational experiences. Joanne's clients include *American Honda Motor Co., Fannie Mae, Opis Management Resources, American Bankers Association, American Psychiatric Association, Maryland Aviation Administration, Sandy Spring Bank,* and many other notable organizations.

A noted author, Joanne's books are used by companies all over the country. Her focus is on providing practical approaches for sustainable organizational renewal through collaboration, skillful leadership and superior customer service. Joanne is the author of *Coaching: The Lost Leadership Art* and *Calamity-Free Collaboration: Making Teamwork WORK!* Her articles are featured in magazines, journals and trade publications, including:: *At Your Service; HR Now; Recharger Magazine; Office Technology Magazine; Forum; Source; Florida HR Review;* and *Support World*. Get complimentary copies of Joanne's articles at www.smiklespeaks.com.

Watch for the release of Joanne's latest book, *The Art & Science of Coaching*.

Index